Fruits

peaches

oranges

strawberries

grapes

blueberries

kiwis

bananas

watermelons

What fruit
do you like?

I like bananas.

What fruit
do you like?

I like peaches.

What fruit do you like?

I like watermelons.

Word List

peaches

oranges

strawberries

grapes

blueberries

kiwis

bananas

watermelons